W9-BRM-755

Dedication

GARDEN MAGIC is dedicated to my Facebook friends
whose "likes" and comments led to the image choices…
and specifically to my mother and my sister,
without whom I would be less than whole.

www.facebook.com/phillipwatsondesigns